RACIAL BIAS:
IS CHANGE POSSIBLE?

Barbara Diggs

ReferencePoint
Press

San Diego, CA

About the Author

Barbara Diggs is the author of multiple nonfiction books for middle school students. A Washington, DC, native, she currently lives in Paris, France, with her family.

For more information, contact:
ReferencePoint Press, Inc.
PO Box 27779
San Diego, CA 92198
www.ReferencePointPress.com

Picture Credits:
Cover: melitas/Shutterstock Images

6: Associated Press
10: UPI/Alamy Stock Photo
14: wundervisuals/iStock
16: Kzenon/Shutterstock
19: Pierre-Jean Durieu/Alamy Stock Photo
21: FatCamera/iStock
25: mimagephotography/Shutterstock

29: Associated Press
31: Monkey Business Images/Shutterstock
36: Rocketclips, Inc./Shutterstock
40: CLIPAREA I Custom media/Shutterstock
42: fizkes/Shutterstock
45: Robert Kneschke/Shutterstock
47: bgrocker/Shutterstock
52: Maury Aaseng
54: Steve Vidler/Alamy Stock Photo

LIBRARY OF CONGRESS CATALOGING-IN-PUBLICATION DATA

Names: Diggs, Barbara, author.
Title: Racial bias : is change possible? / by Barbara Diggs.
Description: San Diego, CA : ReferencePoint Press, Inc., 2023. | Includes bibliographical references and index.
Identifiers: LCCN 2022003593 (print) | LCCN 2022003594 (ebook) | ISBN 9781678203504 (library binding) | ISBN 9781678203511 (ebook)
Subjects: LCSH: Race discrimination--United States--Juvenile literature. | Racism--United States--Juvenile literature. | African Americans--Social conditions--Juvenile literature.
Classification: LCC E184.A1 D456 2023 (print) | LCC E184.A1 (ebook) | DDC 305.800973--dc23/eng/20220309
LC record available at https://lccn.loc.gov/2022003593
LC ebook record available at https://lccn.loc.gov/2022003594

CONTENTS

AN INSIDIOUS HARM

On April 12, 2018, two Black entrepreneurs, Rashon Nelson and Donte Robinson, went to a Starbucks in a well-to-do area of Philadelphia to attend a business meeting with a real estate developer. The pair arrived several minutes early, and Nelson asked the Starbucks barista if he could use the restroom. She told him that it was for paying customers only, so Nelson sat down with Robinson to wait for their business associate.

Moments later, the Starbucks manager approached them and asked if they needed anything. They declined, informing her that they were waiting for their associate. The manager told them they needed to make a purchase or leave. Surprised, they politely refused, repeating that they were waiting for someone. The manager immediately called the police.

To the shock of the two men—and others present in Starbucks—multiple police officers showed up and arrested Nelson and Robinson for trespassing and creating a disturbance. Although video evidence shows the two men had not been disruptive and had spoken calmly to the officers, they were placed in handcuffs and jailed.

Outrage Spreads

As Nelson and Robinson sat in jail, anger was brewing on their behalf. A Starbucks patron, Melissa DePino, recorded the incident on her cell phone and uploaded it to Twitter with the accompanying message: "The police were called because these men hadn't ordered anything. They were waiting for a friend to show, who did as they were taken out in handcuffs for doing nothing. All the other white ppl are wondering why it's never happened to us when we do the same thing."[1]

The video immediately went viral. Over the next few days, thousands of people decried the incident as a stark example of racial bias. Starbucks and the police had treated Nelson and Robinson differently than White people in similar circumstances because the two men were Black.

> "The police were called because these men hadn't ordered anything. They were waiting for a friend to show, who did as they were taken out in handcuffs for doing nothing. All the other white ppl are wondering why it's never happened to us when we do the same thing."[1]
>
> —Melissa DePino, Starbucks patron

Even the Starbucks organization agreed that racial bias was at play. A few days after the incident, Starbucks chief executive officer Kevin Johnson personally apologized to Nelson and Robinson. He also issued a letter stating that the manager was wrong to call the police in this situation and that the organization "stands firmly against discrimination and racial profiling."[2] The following month, the coffee chain closed eight thousand stores for one day to give anti–racial bias training to its staff to prevent similar situations.

The good news is that this distressing incident had positive outcomes. Though shaken and humiliated, Nelson and Robinson were released without being charged. They worked out a private settlement with Starbucks and persuaded the City of Philadelphia to create a $200,000 financial literacy program for underprivileged children.

The bad news is that countless incidents of racial bias continue to happen every day. Most of these occurrences go unacknowledged and do not have favorable resolutions. While each individual incident of bias may seem small, when taken together they give rise to immense racial inequalities and injustices and create deep social rifts.

Rashon Nelson, left, and Donte Robinson, right, were arrested in 2018 while waiting for a business associate in a Philadelphia Starbucks. Their arrest increased public awareness of racial bias. Here they sit on their attorney's sofa following a press interview.

What Is Bias Anyway?

In general, a bias is a preference for or prejudice against a particular thing, person, or group. Biases can be conscious or unconscious, positive or negative, harmless or dangerous, easy to identify or subtle. But no matter their form, we all have them, and they affect how we see the world.

A conscious bias (also known as explicit bias) is a preference that we're aware we have. For example, you might have a conscious bias toward a certain flavor of ice cream or sports team. You know that given the option, you're always going to choose, say, chocolate chip ice cream or root for your local football team, even if they're terrible.

By contrast, an unconscious bias (implicit bias) is a preference or prejudice that we're not aware we have. You might have an unwitting preference for sitting on the left side of the classroom rather than the right, for instance. Or you might unconsciously avoid someone in your class who, deep down, reminds you of a childhood bully.

Biases become harmful when they lead us to treat people unfairly. When unfair treatment of a particular group is widespread in a community or society, it gives rise to discrimination and inequality. Many groups in our society—including women, the LGBTQ community, the disabled community, and obese people—have suffered from pervasive bias. But due to the country's long history of racially discriminatory laws, policies, and social codes, racial bias stands out as a particularly entrenched and destructive problem.

How Racial Bias Affects Our Society

Like any other bias, racial bias can be conscious or unconscious. Conscious racial bias occurs when individuals acknowledge (even if only to themselves) a preference for people of their racial group or prejudice against other racial groups. We can easily understand the harm caused by people with explicit racial biases, since their attitudes and actions plainly perpetuate racial discrimination and injustice.

The more insidious problem is implicit racial bias. Implicit racial bias occurs when people demonstrate a racial preference or prejudice without intending to or realizing it. Their actions are not based on conscious prejudicial feelings but arise from subconscious stereotypical perceptions of a racial group. Implicit bias is even more pervasive than explicit bias and just as damaging. Yet many people don't want to believe that it applies to them. They insist that they would know if they had such biases or were acting prejudicially.

Statistics suggest otherwise. For example, one study revealed that on an eBay auction of iPods, in which researchers alternated the skin color of the hand holding the device in the ad, the White hand holding the iPod received 21 percent more offers than the Black hand, despite all other factors being equal. Other studies have shown that people with White-sounding names are considerably more likely (sometimes as much as 50 percent more) to receive a call back from potential employers, landlords, professors, or state representatives than people with African American–sounding names, even when all other aspects were equalized.

While some of these people may have made consciously biased decisions, many would probably sincerely object to the idea that racial preference influenced their decision-making. But the imbalanced results speak for themselves: many people have a preference for Whiteness or a bias against Blackness in a range of situations, whether they realize it or not.

Scores of studies show that implicit racial bias rears its head in virtually all critical aspects of life: employment, education, medicine, criminal justice, housing, and wages. Naturally, racial biases affect not only African Americans but Latinos, Asian Americans, and Native Americans as well. All minority groups experiencing racial bias have significant and harmful disparities in one or more of these areas.

What Can We Do About Implicit Racial Bias?

Implicit racial bias is a serious and complex issue. It can negatively affect our decisions, behaviors, and judgment and can produce compounding harms. The problem is further complicated because many people are afraid to acknowledge their own implicit biases because they fear it means they're racist. But having biases doesn't make you a bad person or racist. In fact, the implicit biases we have about race usually do not align with our conscious beliefs about race. "Think of implicit bias as the thumbprint of culture on our brain," says social psychologist Mahzarin Banaji, cocreator of the term *implicit bias*. "We carry it around with us and we don't even know that we have it. And yet it emerges."[3]

The truth is that everyone—of every racial group—has unconscious racial biases. Implicit bias is pervasive in our society. Can we ever get rid of it? The answer is: Probably not entirely. But with collective action, we can reduce it enough to make society more equitable. The first step is understanding it. That means knowing how implicit biases arise, what their adverse effects are, and how to recognize and counter our own biases. This work isn't easy but is crucial for a healthy, more just society.

CHAPTER ONE

The Roots of Bias

Being biased isn't entirely our fault. The extraordinary efficiency of the human brain is partly to blame. Our brain is bombarded with around 11 million sensory impressions at any given moment—shapes, colors, sounds, objects, temperatures, movements, scents, emotions, tastes—but our conscious mind can only process a fraction of that, about fifty bits of information per second. To make sense of this deluge, the brain immediately sorts the information into categories and patterns based on prior knowledge and associations. When it needs to make decisions drawn from this massive data pool, the brain often uses shortcuts—called heuristics by scientists—to simplify the decision-making process.

We frequently rely on shortcuts without realizing it. When information is missing, our brain fills in gaps with what it presumes to be correct. That's why we can *raed misspelld wrds wiithot skpping ai beat*. The brain automatically seeks familiar or expected patterns to arrive at the most probable conclusion. These shortcuts work well the vast majority of the time. We don't have to calculate an oncoming car's exact speed and trajectory to know to jump out of its path. We don't puzzle over the purpose of a chair every time we see a different model.

But the brain doesn't always get things right. Sometimes its quick reliance on shortcuts leads to irrational or inaccurate conclusions. To be efficient, it often reaches for the fastest or easiest answer rather than taking the time to consider what is logical or true. It might even push aside pertinent information in its haste to reach a simpler, though flawed, conclusion. When we use such faulty shortcuts to categorize people, it can lead to stereotyping and bias.

Shortcuts Gone Wrong

In the early 1970s psychologists Daniel Kahneman and Amos Tversky conducted a series of studies designed to identify certain mental shortcuts we use and to illustrate how these shortcuts can lead to irrational judgments. In one of their most well-known studies, the researchers asked study participants to guess the *most likely* field of study of a fictional graduate student, "Tom W."

When study participants had no information about Tom other than the size of different fields of study at Tom's university, they

Psychologist Daniel Kahneman is pictured in 2013 receiving the Presidential Medal of Freedom for his work in behavioral economics. Studies by Kahneman and psychologist Amos Tversky helped reveal the way that mental shortcuts lead to irrational judgments.

were most likely to guess that Tom was a student in the most populated field, humanities. They were unlikely to choose one of the smaller fields, like computer science or engineering, because it was statistically more likely that Tom would be among the many students in the largest study field rather than a small one.

However, the participants guessed differently when the researchers provided a psychological profile of Tom. They described him as a highly intelligent and orderly person who had a taste for science fiction and corny puns but didn't enjoy interacting with other people. With this information, the participants overwhelmingly and consistently guessed that Tom was studying computer science or engineering. This guess was much less rational, because Tom was still statistically more likely to be in the largest study field. Yet even participants well versed in statistics ignored this fact.

Kahneman and Tversky concluded that humans are biased to make judgments through "representativeness" or stereotype. When quickly assessing whether someone (or something) fits into a specific category, the brain's impulse is to reach for the simplicity of a stereotype or an overgeneralization to determine whether there's a match. This occurrence is known as the representativeness bias.

In this case, Tom's description fit the stereotype of a socially awkward, science-minded individual, so participants chose a field of study that matched their perception of him. They made this choice even though it was statistically unlikely that he'd be in that field and even though they'd been asked to guess his *most* likely field. The easy lure of the stereotype pushed out more logical considerations.

Shortcuts in the Real World

An *Atlantic* magazine article published in 2017 told a story that illustrates how shortcuts such as the representativeness bias can work against people of color. The article told of an African American woman—a college graduate and head bank teller—who was passed over for a management training program at the bank. Her

White male colleague, who only had a high school diploma, was invited to participate.

When the woman asked her manager why her less-qualified colleague was referred to the management program and she wasn't, her manager revealed his bias without hesitation: "He reminded me of myself when I was just starting out," he told her. "He just looked like a banker."[4]

As this example shows, reliance on shortcuts can keep people of color from advancing and can lead to racial disparities. The manager's stereotypical vision of a banking manager as a White male clearly influenced his decision to help the White colleague advance up the corporate ladder. He may not have intended to prevent an African American woman from entering management nor consciously thought, "This Black woman doesn't look like a banker" as he made his decision. Nonetheless, his reflexive preference for Whiteness and maleness had the same discriminatory effect.

Repeated use of shortcuts can create mental ruts. That is, we can become so accustomed to thinking about an issue in a certain way that it becomes deeply entrenched and difficult to think about in any other way. For example, if a person regularly envisions banking managers as White men, it may become hard for them to think of banking managers as anything but White men.

Such a rut can not only prevent a biased person from hiring people who don't meet the bank manager stereotype, it may lead him or her to take a bank manager who falls outside the stereotype less seriously. They may devalue the nonconforming individual's valid opinions and inflate their shortcomings, never consciously realizing how bias has colored their perspective. As cognitive scientist Art Markman notes, "People are biased to interpret . . . evidence in ways that are consistent with their desires."[5]

In-Group Favoritism

Social psychologists theorize that bias also arises because of a primal preference for people with whom we share an identity. Evolutionarily, this preference makes sense. Our prehistoric

Fast vs. Slow Thinking

In his groundbreaking book, *Thinking Fast and Slow*, Daniel Kahneman describes the brain as having two methods of processing information: System 1 and System 2.

System 1 refers to the brain's automatic thought process. We use this system when we wander home from school without thinking about it or when completing the phrase "bread and . . . " System 1 also kicks in when we're reacting to a perceived threat or when our emotions are spiraling out of control.

System 2 is a slower, more deliberate and more orderly process in which we apply reason. We use this process when we make a conscious mental effort, such as when multiplying 37 x 41 or looking for the best seat in a movie theater. It's also the system at work when we exercise self-control over emotions or actions.

Under Kahneman's framework, we use System 1 when we make snap judgments about people based on stereotypes. But we can decide to employ System 2 to overrule the impulses and associations of System 1, avoid stereotyping, and make more rational decisions.

ancestors learned that belonging to a group dramatically increased their chance of survival. Groups offered security, assistance, and care in an uncertain and dangerous world. People relied on group members for these benefits and expected the same in return.

Outsiders usually posed a threat to precious resources such as food and shelter or carried the risk of introducing a new infectious disease. Our ancestors, therefore, developed not only a preference for those in their own group but also a strong suspicion of strangers. If someone different approached your cave, it was smarter to assume he or she meant harm. Having prejudice against outsiders thus provided an evolutionary advantage. Sociologists call the group with whom we identify an in-group and those with whom we don't an out-group.

A group of soccer players huddle together. Since prehistoric times, humans have liked belonging to groups, and research shows that group members usually show favorable bias toward members of their own group.

Fast-forward to modern times; humans still like belonging to groups, and we continue to show bias toward in-group members over others. But we demonstrate this preference even when survival or valuable resources aren't on the line. In most cases, we show a preference to anyone in our same group, whether that group is formed by race, ethnicity, class, grade, dog ownership, or cola preference. Studies have even shown that people are favorably biased toward members of groups they identify with when assigned to a random group.

Why do humans so persistently display in-group favoritism? Experts offer multiple theories. An exaggerated instinct for self-protection can play a role, as can hope for reciprocal favorable treatment from others in our group. But most experts agree that in-group bias strongly relates to self-esteem. Belonging to a group usually gives us a positive social identity and a sense of self-worth. We are biased toward members because we want to see them, and thus ourselves, as valued and special.

Not only do we tend to show preferential treatment to in-group members, we often inflate the perceived value of the group even more by seeing the group as having particularly favorable attributes (for example: *The kids in our ninth-grade class are all super smart!*). Problems arise, however, if we seek to inflate the group's value by disparaging other groups (for example: *That other ninth-grade class has all the dumb losers*). We can start to believe the stories we tell ourselves about others without regard for truth or accuracy.

We're especially likely to put others down when feeling bad about ourselves. "[Low self-esteem] is one of the oldest accounts of why people stereotype and have prejudice: It makes us feel better about ourselves,"[6] says Jeffrey Sherman, a social psychologist at the University of California, Davis.

> "[Low self-esteem] is one of the oldest accounts of why people stereotype and have prejudice: It makes us feel better about ourselves."[6]
>
> —Jeffrey Sherman, social psychologist

Implicit Out-Group Bias

Though we may not realize it, our brain assesses every person we encounter and makes immediate decisions about whether each one belongs to one of our in-groups or to an out-group. In making this decision, our brain draws information from a person's observable characteristics and marks of identity: skin color, physical features, language, accents, religious indicators, clothing, and so forth. It matches these observations with previous experiences and associations and then categorizes the person. Once we recognize the person as an in-group or out-group member, we have an idea of how to behave toward them.

This process usually occurs in the blink of an eye as the brain—not wanting to take the slow, analytical route—shortcuts to the representativeness bias. This quick assessment can make us stereotype the individual, which, in turn, can lead to massive overgeneralizations, incorrect conclusions, and unfair treatment.

Our impulsive categorization of people, paired with the brain's stereotype shortcut, helps explain the mental process that gives rise to implicit racial bias. This is what's likely happening when a hiring manager shows an unconscious preference for White-sounding names, a traveler becomes fearful when overhearing a person speaking Arabic on an airplane, or a person of color acts curt and mistrustful when a White person enters his or her space. In these situations, we see people solely as stereotypical representatives of an out-group rather than as individuals. These reactions do not necessarily mean that we're prejudiced or racist but that we harbor stereotypical associations in our subconscious. Fortunately, we can overrule this.

Stepping Away from Stereotypes

Our brains are hardwired to categorize information, but we don't have to accept it when the brain assigns a stereotype to someone, nor do we have to let it dictate our actions. "Human beings have

A young man sits at a job interview. The brain's tendency to quickly stereotype other people can lead to implicit racial bias, such as when a hiring manager shows an unconscious preference for White-sounding names.

A Class Divided

A famous two-day experiment shows how quickly we can form in-group biases and out-group prejudices. In 1968 Jane Elliott, an Iowa schoolteacher seeking to teach her all-White class about discrimination, divided them by eye color. On the first day, Elliott told the class that blue-eyed kids were superior to those with brown eyes—smarter, neater, nicer—and gave them special privileges, such as a longer recess. Meanwhile, she made the brown-eyed children wear collars and criticized and ridiculed them. The next day Elliott told the kids she'd made a mistake—the brown-eyed group were actually the "superior" ones.

The results shocked Elliott. On their respective days, the children of the dominant group quickly became nasty and abusive to their classmates, calling them stupid, refusing to play with them, and bossing them around. The favored group also performed better in school, while the unfavored group began to perform worse. Tears were shed, but Elliott's point was made: the children learned that people shouldn't be judged on appearances. The experiment has since taught countless others how environmental cues can lead us to form strong biases and prejudices, even when based on characteristics that have no inherent significance.

the ability to learn to associate two things together very quickly—that is innate. What we teach ourselves, what we choose to associate is up to us,"[7] says social psychologist Mahzarin Banaji.

In other words, many of the associations we've learned can be unlearned. By consciously engaging our rational mind, we can counter biased responses to stereotypical associations and try to form new associations. Integral to this process is understanding where implicit stereotypes come from and why they make a formidable impression on our subconscious.

> "Human beings have the ability to learn to associate two things together very quickly—that is innate. What we teach ourselves, what we choose to associate is up to us."[7]
>
> —Mahzarin Banaji, social psychologist

CHAPTER TWO

How Implicit Bias Develops

When social justice advocate Debby Irving was five years old, she became fascinated with Indians. At her local library, an intriguing mural featuring three dark-skinned, feather-wearing indigenous Americans standing with a handful of colonists always captured her gaze. She began reading about early Native American life, imagining herself riding horses or living in a tepee. But one day Irving realized that she'd never heard of any modern Native Americans. So she asked her mother what had happened to them.

Her mother shook her head. "They drank too much,"[8] she responded. She then assured her daughter that although they were lovely people, they were ruined by their inability to handle alcohol. She went on to tell her daughter a story of a Native American who went on a drunken rampage and killed several children with an ax. Horrified and disappointed, Irving's interest in Native Americans began to wane.

At no point did her mother refer to race or skin color, but Irving says the story nonetheless "whispered to [her] that Indians were somehow 'other,' like a whole separate and inferior species."[9] After this conversation, she began to develop a negative stereotypical image of the group—images confirmed by the media, which depicted Native Americans as so-called violent savages who ran around whooping and scalping White people. Irving says she began to slowly and subtly believe that she, as a White person, was "of a superior race and wholly disconnected from other races—except as a potential victim."[10]

Today Irving recognizes that her views were built on one-sided misinformation. She'd heard nothing of how the colonists intentionally introduced alcohol to Native Americans to take advantage of them. Neither did she hear stories of the colonists' violence against and cruelty toward indigenous people. But she doesn't blame her mother for being misleading—her mother hadn't known the truth either. Neither of them had thought to question the representation of Native Americans that seemed set in stone by teachers, books, movies, and images. "I took it all at face value, constructing for myself a one-dimensional world in which people were right or wrong, good or bad, like me or not,"[11] she says.

Dancers celebrate Native American culture at the United Tribes International Powwow in Bismarck, North Dakota. Stereotypes blind us to the humanity and individuality of other people and cultures.

Bias Sponges

Like Irving, we begin to form racial biases as young children, usually through information picked up from our family and environment. Although some people deliberately pass on racist or bigoted attitudes, many who deliver biased messages to kids don't necessarily have bad intentions. Some pass along false or incomplete information about other racial groups out of ignorance, never fully realizing that they're perpetuating stereotypes and bias, nor that they're communicating implicit messages about a racial hierarchy or White supremacy. But even very young kids are masters at detecting these unspoken subtleties.

Kids generally start demonstrating racial bias based on social cues around age four or five. Although babies as young as six months old may show a preference for their own racial group, this is most likely due to limited exposure to other races. Toddlers around age two or three interact with peers without showing particular racial bias. But just before kindergarten, things change: preschoolers begin to show a preference for their own racial group and display other racial biases. Social psychologists believe this may partly occur because, as put by psychologist Danielle Perszyk, at this age, kids become "increasingly attuned to social category labels, social status, and biases exhibited by family members."[12]

To determine how social cues influence preschoolers, a team of psychologists conducted a study in which four- and five-year-olds watched a video of a social interaction between three people. In the video, a woman spoke with one person in a warm, pleasant manner and used welcoming mannerisms but talked to the other person using a cold and disapproving tone and a standoffish attitude. All people in the video were of the same race.

When the researchers asked the children which of the two persons spoken to they liked best, a large majority preferred the person who was spoken to approvingly. The kids were also more likely to use a new word if used by the person who'd received positive feedback, more likely to want to share a toy with that person, and even preferred a friend of that person.

Researchers have found that when a teacher gives positive feedback—such as a smile—to certain students, other students often perceive those students as smarter than students who do not receive positive feedback.

In another study, slightly older children (ages five to eight) observed how a teacher treated two randomly separated groups of kids. The teacher gave positive nonverbal feedback, such as smiles and nods, to one group but not the other. When the researchers asked the child observers which group was smarter, the kids consistently chose the group that had received the positive signals, even though there was no objective evidence of the group being smarter. "This means that observing even just a single interaction with a member of a group could lead children to develop biases," explains Allison Skinner, the lead researcher on the first study. "This implies that observing a parent or teacher [who] seems a little less friendly toward a Black person than they usually are toward White people has the potential to produce biases."[13]

Bombarded by the Media

The media play an especially commanding role in forming our implicit biases. Newspapers, television shows, films, news programs,

The Danger of an Image

Stereotypical racial images in the media can strengthen both implicit and explicit bias. When COVID-19 first hit New York in March 2020, several New York news outlets used generic photographs of masked Asians and Chinatown to accompany the stories. None of the photos were taken in the context of the coronavirus, nor did the images feature people discussed in the article.

Although the newspapers may not have had ill intent, using stereotypical images such as these pushed the narrative that all Asian people are responsible for the coronavirus. The Asian American Journalists Association (AAJA) called on newspapers to stop using photos of Asians or Chinatown unrelated to the coronavirus when writing articles about the disease.

"It further stokes unnecessary and unfounded fears about COVID-19, and negatively affects the safety and well-being of members of the Asian American community," says Naomi Tacuyan Underwood, executive director of AAJA.

Anti-Asian hate incidents have spiked since the start of the pandemic. The Stop AAPI Hate advocacy group reports that from March 19, 2020, through June 2021, Asian Americans reported over nine thousand hateful incidents, ranging from taunts to violent assaults. Some of these incidents were related to or prompted by the victim wearing a face mask.

Quoted in Natasha Roy, "News Outlets Criticized for Using Chinatown Photos in Coronavirus Articles," NBC News, March 6, 2020. www.nbcnews.com.

and advertisements regularly feature stereotyped portrayals of different races or deliver persistently negative or one-sided messages about a particular racial group. When we see these generalized depictions over and over, they become rooted in our subconscious. Even if we know them to be inaccurate or oversimplified on a conscious level, we often unthinkingly rely on them when making rapid assessments.

Jennifer L. Eberhardt could hardly believe it when she saw this bias at work in her own five-year-old. Eberhardt, an African American social psychologist specializing in implicit bias, was boarding an airplane when her son saw a Black man and mentioned that the man looked like his daddy. But what the boy said next stunned her: "I hope that man doesn't rob the plane." Eberhardt tried to speak calmly as she said, "You know Daddy wouldn't rob a plane. Why did you say that?" The boy looked troubled and replied, "I don't know why I said that. I don't know why I was *thinking* that."[14]

But Eberhardt understood. "Our ideas about race are shaped by stereotype. And one of the strongest stereotypes in American society associate[s] blacks with criminality," she later wrote in her book, *Biased*. "Even with no malice—even with no hatred—the black-crime association made its way into the mind of my five-year-old son, [as it does] into all of our children, into all of us."[15]

We need not look far to see how the media display African Americans in a negative, stereotypical light with disproportionate frequency. For example, a recent study revealed that Black Americans represent 26 percent of people arrested for crimes, but they appear in 37 percent of news stories about crime. However, White Americans make up 77 percent of crime suspects yet only appear as criminals in the news media 28 percent of the time. The heavy focus on African American crimes—and the underrepresentation of White crime—helps bolster the stereotype that all African Americans are criminal and dangerous.

> "Our ideas about race are shaped by stereotype. And one of the strongest stereotypes in American society associate[s] blacks with criminality. Even with no malice—even with no hatred—the black-crime association made its way into the mind of my five-year-old son, [as it does] into all of our children, into all of us."[15]
>
> —Jennifer L. Eberhardt, social psychologist

The media also consistently paint a misleading picture of African Americans as poor and financially dependent on the government. An analysis of a random sample of television, print, and online news stories for a two-year period found that Black people were featured or depicted in 59 percent of the news stories about the poor, although that racial group makes up 22 percent of the poor population. In contrast, White Americans only appeared in 17 percent of the news stories, even though they make up 66 percent of the poor population. These vast disparities lead us to associate Black people, but not White people, with poverty.

Latinos face similar exaggerated representations. One analysis found that 66 percent of news stories featuring Latinos focused either on crime or immigration. Another study revealed that, over a ten-year period, images of Latinos appeared in a whopping 75.9 percent of stories on immigration, although Latinos make up just over half of the national immigrant population. The same study revealed that 54 percent of the photos accompanying these stories featured undocumented immigrants— more than double the percentage of the undocumented immigrant population in the United States.

The press's tendency to link Latinos to immigration and undocumented immigrants may be why many Americans overestimate the number of undocumented Latino immigrants in the United States. Only about 13 percent of the Latino immigrant population is undocumented. Yet a 2021 poll conducted by collaborating Latino groups found that Americans of all racial backgrounds estimate the group's undocumented rate as 30 to 39 percent. Such misperceptions are likely to enhance a negative bias against Latinos.

Hollywood's Impact

Few would be surprised that stereotypical depictions of people of color in movies and films have greatly added to implicit racial bias. Although Hollywood now makes an effort to cast minorities in diverse roles, African Americans and Latinos have been overwhelmingly cast as criminals, drug pushers and addicts, servants, or menial workers throughout Hollywood's history. Asians and Native Americans, too, have been repeatedly depicted in stereotypical or offensive roles for several decades.

White actors tend to be the hero of a film or series. Even when they're not, their characters have a full range of individual traits and backgrounds, just as people do in real life. Such im-

Researchers have found that television can cause lower self-esteem in children of color.

balanced representation not only prompts our subconscious to perceive minorities as negative stereotypes but also primes us to see White people in a positive light by contrast.

This disparity can have a particularly enormous impact on children. Studies have shown that watching television can lower self-esteem in children of color and White girls but raise self-esteem in White boys. "Much like adults, what children see [on screens] is what they believe the world really is," says clinical psychologist Allison Briscoe-Smith. "As children continually see certain messages about who's in power, or how people are treated, it becomes part of the information that they use to understand how the world works."[16]

> "Much like adults, what children see [on screens] is what they believe the world really is. As children continually see certain messages about who's in power, or how people are treated, it becomes part of the information that they use to understand how the world works."[16]
>
> —Allison Briscoe-Smith, clinical psychologist

Coded Language

Implicit racial bias can also arise from the language used to describe people from a particular racial group. "Regardless of our intentions, the language we use may implicitly or explicitly transmit bias in the form of stereotypes and prejudice," says Lauren Ann McDonough Lebois of Harvard Medical School. For example, US media outlets frequently use *thug* to describe male African American suspects in violent crimes (or even sometimes African American victims of violence), conjuring an unforgiving image of an immoral person. Yet many White people accused of equally violent crimes are usually described in more sympathetic terms, such as *loner* or *a troubled history* or *mentally unstable*.

As media outlets repeat such words and terms, they reinforce the stereotype of African American men as inherently criminal but offer context for Whites who engage in violence. To avoid bias, we need to pay attention to how people of different races are described in the media and notice how such language shifts our perspective.

Quoted in Jennifer Knudsen, "How to Find Prejudice Hidden in Our Words," Greater Good, October 16, 2016. https://greatergood.berkeley.edu.

Fear of Darkness

In societies worldwide, darkness is linked to wickedness, wrongdoing, and negativity. Villains are often portrayed wearing black clothing. Most crimes are perceived to take place under cover of darkness. Death is usually associated with the color black. Social psychologists believe that these negative associations with darkness contribute to our implicit bias against people with a darker skin tone—regardless of race—and unconsciously perceive them as more menacing or immoral.

Through a series of studies, researchers at New York University did indeed find that people link dark skin tone with bad behavior. The first two studies analyzed online articles of celebrities and politicians. The researchers found that the darker the skin tone of the person in the image accompanying the article, the more negative or critical the story. In the second study, participants who had watched grainy video surveillance images of a crime were more likely to identify suspects in artificially darkened photos over suspects in lighter photos.

The researchers noted that an association between color and morality could have serious implications, particularly in criminal justice. Judges, juries, and police officers may be biased against darker-skinned suspects accused of a crime, or eyewitnesses might be more likely to misidentify suspects with darker skin simply because of their color.

Unfortunately, studies bear out the researchers' concerns. One study led by Eberhardt showed that African American men convicted of murder are significantly more likely to receive the death penalty if they have stereotypically "Black" facial features— dark skin, broad nose, thick lips—than are light-skinned or White men. Other investigations show that lighter-skinned Black women receive notably more lenient sentences than darker-skinned women, and dark-skinned youth are more likely to be targeted in stop-and-frisks (stopped, questioned, and searched by police) than their light-skinned counterparts. Some social scientists are calling for further research into this area and for policy makers to address the implicit bias against dark-skinned individuals in the justice system.

CHAPTER THREE

The Destructive Effects of Implicit Racial Bias

By all accounts, Elijah McClain was a sweet, gentle soul, though a bit different. A massage therapist in Aurora, Colorado, the twenty-three-year-old was known to play his violin to shelter animals so they wouldn't feel lonely. One August night in 2019, McClain was walking home from a convenience store, listening to music through his earbuds. Someone in the neighborhood called the police, saying that McClain looked "sketchy"[17] because he was waving his arms as he walked and was wearing an open-faced ski mask. The caller didn't report that McClain was doing anything illegal but did mention that he was Black.

When two police officers showed up, they ordered McClain to stop walking. McClain, who may not have heard the order because of the earbuds, stopped only after they had repeated the order several times. The police quickly restrained him, pinning him against a wall, and then wrestled him to the ground as he struggled, pleaded with the officers, and cried out in pain. They put him in a carotid chokehold, which cuts blood flow to the brain. He drifted in and out of consciousness, vomiting several times.

When the paramedics arrived, they immediately dosed the slender man with a powerful sedative meant for a much heavier person weighing 200 pounds (91 kg). McClain fell unconscious and went into cardiac arrest. He died three days later.

Harsher Consequences

McClain's tragic story is an all-too-familiar example of how implicit racial bias can lead to devastating consequences for people of color. In the criminal justice context, implicit bias is particularly dangerous. It works hand in hand with structural racism to restrict the life and liberty of people of color at disproportionately high rates. Police, prosecutors, juries, and judges are likely to treat people of color with disparate severity. For example, according to the US Sentencing Commission, Blacks and Latinos are more likely to receive longer sentences—sometimes 20 percent longer—than Whites with similar criminal histories who are convicted of the same crimes. With respect to plea bargains, a study by Professor Carlos Berdejó of Loyola Law School found that White defendants are 25 percent more likely than Black defendants to have their most serious crime dismissed and are 75 percent more likely to have misdemeanors that could carry a jail sentence dismissed, dropped, or reduced.

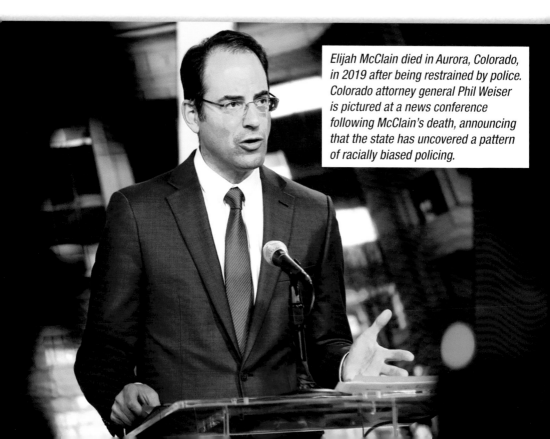

Elijah McClain died in Aurora, Colorado, in 2019 after being restrained by police. Colorado attorney general Phil Weiser is pictured at a news conference following McClain's death, announcing that the state has uncovered a pattern of racially biased policing.

Police shooting statistics show equally glaring disparities. A joint study at Yale University and the University of Pennsylvania found that from 2015 to 2020, armed Native Americans were killed by the police at 3 times the rate of armed Whites, armed Blacks were killed at 2.6 times the rate, and Latinos at 1.3 times the rate. In unarmed encounters, Blacks were killed at 3 times the rate of Whites, while Latinos were killed at 1.45 times the rate. These substantial imbalances indicate that implicit racial bias influences how quick police officers are to fire their guns, particularly with respect to African American men.

Other research supports this view. In a University of Colorado study in which participants made rapid decisions about whether to shoot armed or unarmed individuals in a video game simulation, White participants mistakenly shot unarmed Black avatars faster and more frequently than unarmed White avatars.

A Montclair State University study found that participants perceived photos of the faces and bodies of Black men as larger, stronger, and more muscular than photos of equal-sized White men. Disturbingly, White participants also perceived the Black men in the photos as more capable of causing harm in a confrontation and believed that police would be more entitled to subdue them with force, even if the men were unarmed. Black participants did not hold such views, even if they misperceived the Black men in the photos as being larger.

These findings are significant for understanding why the police are more likely to kill Black men. "Unarmed black men are disproportionately more likely to be shot and killed by police, and often these killings are accompanied by explanations that cite the physical size of the person shot," explains John Wilson, the lead researcher on the study. "Our research suggests that these descriptions may reflect stereotypes of black males that do not seem to comport with reality."[18]

Such bias may have been a factor in McClain's death. The police report described him as having "incredible, crazy strength,"[19] although he only weighed 143 pounds (65 kg) and was smaller

Unconscious bias leads some teachers to react more harshly to nonwhite students even when their behavior is no different from any other student in class. This can have life-changing consequences for those students.

than the officers who apprehended him. He was also given a sedative fit for a man 50 to 60 pounds (22.7 to 27.2 kg) heavier than he. Following McClain's death, the Aurora Police Department was found to have a significant pattern of using excessive force on minorities, especially African Americans.

A Slippery Slope

Implicit bias in the educational system can also trigger disproportionately harsh treatment of students in certain racial groups. Public school teacher Sarah E. Fiarman recognized her own implicit biases after complaining to an African American colleague that a few students of color were having side conversations in her class. She recalls that her colleague asked whether White students were doing the same thing, saying, "Educators . . . frequently notice misbehavior among black students while ignoring the same behavior among white students."[20]

Sure enough, when Fiarman made a conscious effort to observe all her students, she noticed that White students were talking out of turn as well. Stunned, she realized that she'd unconsciously focused on the misbehavior of just one subset of students—a realization that was even more upsetting because she taught

What's Structural Racism?

Structural racism (also called systemic racism) describes the modern policies, practices, and norms embedded in our systems and institutions that reinforce racial inequity. This subtle form of racism is a direct legacy of the overt racism and discrimination that permeated our economic, political, social, and legal systems for centuries.

Homeownership provides a clear example of structural racism. In the 1930s the federal government established the Home Owners' Loan Corporation (HOLC) to guarantee mortgages for Americans and encourage home buying. When the HOLC created maps to indicate the mortgage-worthiness of certain neighborhoods, it drew red lines around Black neighborhoods, designating them hazardous-risk investment areas. From 1930 to 1960, only 1 percent of mortgages nationwide were issued to African Americans.

"Redlining" policies became ingrained in credit institutions' approach to mortgage risk. Many creditors today presume Black people to be high risk, as evidenced by the disparate rates at which Blacks are refused mortgage loans compared to Whites of similar creditworthiness. Structural racism in home buying makes it challenging for Black people to own homes and build intergenerational wealth. Structural racism, in general, makes it harder for people of color to access certain opportunities available to Whites and to participate as equal members of society.

about racism and led an antiracism faculty group. "How could I have read the situation so inaccurately? How could I have shown such bias?"[21] Fiarman wondered.

Fiarman's story of unconscious bias is multiplied in various ways in classrooms across the country. Studies have revealed that teachers react more harshly to Black and Latino students' misbehavior than to that of White students, issuing severe punishments for minor infractions, such as dress code violations or tardiness. Another study indicated that teachers reflexively look for misconduct in Black children, especially boys, even when they aren't displaying problematic behavior.

Such biases can have life-changing consequences for these students. Black, Latino, and Native American students are suspended or expelled from school at two to four times the rate of White students. Suspension from school is the top indicator that a youth will drop out. Those who do drop out are much more likely to be unemployed, become involved in illegal activities, and serve jail time. This slippery downward slope contributes to what is known as the "school-to-prison pipeline."

Barriers to Wealth Building

Centuries of virulent racism and exploitation have harmed people of color in innumerable ways, but few injuries are starker than the disparities in wealth accumulation. Multiple generations of people of color were kept in low-paying jobs, were denied access to quality education, and had little means to buy a home—all of which made it substantially more challenging to accrue wealth.

Statistics from the Survey of Consumer Finances show that in 2019 White families had nearly eight times the wealth of Black families. The median wealth for White families was $188,200, while the median for Black families was $24,100. Latinos and Asian Americans also had substantially lower median wealth than White families, at $36,100 and $85,800, respectively.

Implicit bias plays an important role in sustaining these vast wealth gaps. The biggest opportunity for Americans to build wealth is by owning a home. Homes offer a permanent residence, tax-saving benefits, and financial stability and can be used to generate more wealth, such as when rented out or sold to finance a child's education or another investment. Real estate can also be passed to descendants, giving the next generation a financial leg up.

But for certain racial groups, the home-buying process is fraught with implicit bias and discrimination, making it harder for them to take advantage of this valuable asset. African Americans and Latinos are more likely to be declined for mortgages than Whites and Asian Americans, even when they have similar financial characteristics. When they do receive a loan, African Americans, Latinos, and Native Americans are likely to pay higher interest rates.

There's also evidence that White home buyers receive preferential treatment. At least one study of mortgage applications noted that "credit history irregularities on policy applications were often selectively overlooked in the case of White applicants."[22] This suggests that people of color seeking home loans are under more critical scrutiny than White Americans and are less likely to receive the benefit of the doubt when an objective standard is not met.

Analyses show that this discriminatory treatment of people of color in homeownership largely stems from historical racism and the stereotypical association of certain minorities with risk—and Whiteness with stability. Such bias contributes to significant racial disparities in homeowner rates. According to Statista, as of 2019, 73.3 percent of White Americans own homes compared to 42 percent of African Americans, 47.5 percent of Latinos, 50.8 percent of Native Americans, and 57.7 percent of Asian Americans. This difference puts people of color at a staggering disadvantage when building wealth compared to White Americans.

Implicit bias in employment also plays a significant role in wealth disparities. Black and Latino Americans are underrepresented in high-paying industries such as law, engineering, and technology and in senior positions and executive roles. Although many elements contribute to this disparity, the effect of representativeness bias in hiring processes for more lucrative jobs cannot be underestimated. "If you do something simple like Google 'architects' and you go to the images tab, you're primarily going to see white males," says Jonathan Garland, one of the 2 percent of architects in the United States who are African American. "That's the image, that's the brand, that's the look of an architect."[23]

It's not just skin color that triggers bias. A landmark study showed that hiring employers reviewing résumés were 50 percent more likely to reject candidates with stereotypically Black names than those

> "If you do something simple like Google 'architects' and you go to the images tab, you're primarily going to see white males. That's the image, that's the brand, that's the look of an architect."[23]
>
> —Jonathan Garland, African American architect

RACIAL BIAS IN TECHNOLOGY

Unconscious racial bias even shows itself in technology. For example, pulse oximeters, devices that measure blood oxygen levels by using light transmitted through skin, are substantially less likely to give accurate readings for darker-skinned patients. The inaccuracy has resulted in Black and brown patients failing to receive supplemental oxygen when needed. Similarly, facial recognition technology shows significant error rates for dark-skinned people, particularly darker-skinned females. This inaccuracy becomes particularly concerning in the law enforcement context since this technology is often used by police to match photos to mug shot images.

Experts say the lower effectiveness rate in the oximeter and other technologies can go unnoticed in dark-skinned people when tech designers fail to include sufficient numbers of darker-skinned people in designs and tests. "It is easy to look at a machine and assume that everyone's getting the same experience. But technologies are created and developed by people, and so bias, however inadvertent, can be an issue here too," says Sajid Javid, secretary of health for the United Kingdom.

Quoted in Nicola Davis, "From Oximeters to AI, Where Bias in Technology May Lurk," *The Guardian* (Manchester, UK), November, 21, 2021. www.theguardian.com.

with White-sounding names, even when the candidates were equally qualified for the position. Another study found that software engineering job applicants with Mexican-Spanish accents were considered less suitable for the position than those applicants with American-English accents and were seen as less likely to be promoted to management positions.

Asian Americans, although well represented in high-income industries, are still sharply underrepresented in managerial and executive roles, dampening the group's wealth levels. Asian Americans make up 13 percent of the workforce, but only 6 percent are senior executives and managers. Diversity experts believe this disparity is linked to stereotypical perceptions of Asian Americans as unassertive, which runs contrary to the stereotypical American vision of a strong leader.

Hurting Health

Unconscious racial bias can even cause health providers to treat people of color with less care and attention than White people. According to a 2002 National Academies' Institute of Medicine report, "Racial and ethnic minorities tend to receive lower-quality health care than whites do, even when insurance status, income, age, and severity of conditions are comparable."[24] The organization found that people of color are less likely to receive appropriate cardiac care, kidney dialysis, or transplants than their White counterparts or to receive top treatments for cancer or strokes. Numerous subsequent studies have supported these findings.

Most health care professionals believe that they treat every patient with equal care. Yet, a study led by researchers at the University of Colorado, Boulder found that two out of three physicians had an implicit bias against African Americans and Latinos. That bias can influence their actions in subtle ways. For example, there's evidence that White doctors tend to spend less time with patients of color. Some speak in a more dominant or condescending tone to people of color or have a less compassionate demeanor. Some medical providers even give patients of color

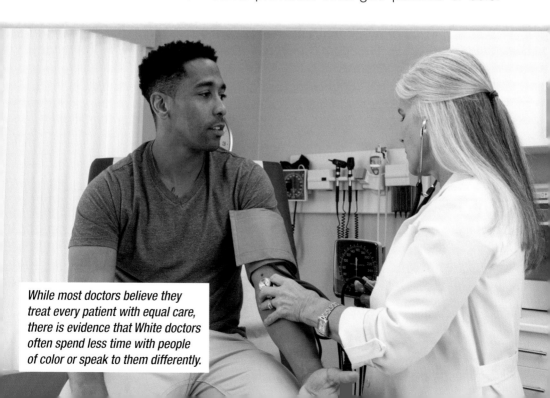

While most doctors believe they treat every patient with equal care, there is evidence that White doctors often spend less time with people of color or speak to them differently.

less effective or less desirable treatments because they unconsciously believe that the patients will be unlikely to comply with more effective treatment protocols.

Such differential treatment contributes to health disparities along racial lines. Black Americans and Latinos have higher rates of hypertension, diabetes, and obesity than other racial groups. African Americans and Native Americans have shorter life expectancies. Asian Americans have the highest liver and stomach cancer rates in the country. They're also more likely than other races to die of these diseases, although these cancers are considered among the most preventable.

The Psychological Toll

Implicit racial bias takes a heavy mental toll on people of color, leading to higher stress levels, depression, and sleep difficulties. It can even trigger physical issues such as headaches and high blood pressure. "The experience of having to question whether something happened to you because of your race or constantly being on edge because your environment is hostile can often leave people feeling invisible, silenced, angry, and resentful,"[25] says Joy Bradford, founder of the mental health platform Therapy for Black Girls.

One of the most psychologically damaging forms of implicit racial bias is microaggressions. These are comments, insults, and offensive actions that many people of color contend with daily. Examples include complimenting an Asian American on their English, telling an African American that they're a credit to their race, or asking a Hispanic American where they're *really* from. Slights such as these unconsciously reveal negative, racially biased beliefs. Although these offhand comments may seem trivial to those who don't experience them, they are emotionally exhausting for people of color, who experience them constantly.

CHAPTER FOUR

Is Implicit Racial Bias Hardwired?

Kettisha, a teacher, was making copies in the teacher's lounge when she overheard what appeared to be an African American consultant speaking with another teacher in Spanish. Listening to them converse, Kettisha remarked to another teacher near the copy machine that she had thought the consultant was Black. Kettisha recalls that as she finished her copies and started to leave the room, the consultant smiled at her and said, "I heard you at the copy machine, and I am black. And, I speak Spanish." Kettisha immediately apologized for her biased assumption. "Not a proud moment," she wrote about the incident later. "But I have never made another assumption about what language a person may or may not speak based on their race."[26]

Can we really abolish implicit bias from one moment to the next, as Kettisha describes? Or are certain associations and neural pathways too ingrained to be truly overcome? These questions have been topics of national conversation for the past several years. Some people believe that implicit racial bias is hardwired. They think that because our brain is naturally designed to categorize and make split-second decisions based on stereotypes, there's nothing we can do to change that impulse or those subconscious associations.

But science indicates that even if we are programmed for bias, we aren't for prejudice. "Our prejudices are not inevitable; they are actually quite malleable, shaped by an ever-changing mix of cultural beliefs and social circumstances,"[27] says Susan Fiske, a social psychologist

"Our prejudices are not inevitable; they are actually quite malleable, shaped by an ever-changing mix of cultural beliefs and social circumstances."[27]

—Susan Fiske, social psychologist

at Princeton University. Other scientists, such as Mina Cikara and Jay Van Bavel, are even more direct: "Race-based prejudice and discrimination . . . are created and reinforced by many social factors, but they are not inevitable consequences of our biology."[28] In other words, implicit racial bias can diminish or change with social circumstances. To understand how and why this is possible, we must once again look at how the human brain functions.

Eyes on the Amygdala

If implicit racial bias could be said to be physically located anywhere, one might say it's in the tiny almond-shaped structure in the brain called the amygdala. Present in each lobe, the amygdala is known as the brain's emotional control and social-decision-making center. It helps us process strong feelings, from happiness to sadness, and plays a central role in making rapid-fire assessments in situations that make us fearful. When we unexpectedly spot a large spider, for example, the amygdala registers it before any other part of the brain and quickly sounds the alarm to react.

The amygdala has a particular connection to implicit racial bias. In 2000 researchers using functional magnetic resonance imaging (fMRI) to map brain activity found that White subjects showed enhanced amygdala activity upon seeing pictures of unfamiliar Black men. The researchers noticed that the degree of amygdala activity was directly correlated to the participants' scores on a test measuring their implicit racial bias. In other words, the higher their implicit bias score on the test, the more amygdala activation they showed.

Numerous fMRI studies have shown comparable results. For example, a study conducted by Fiske and colleagues found greater

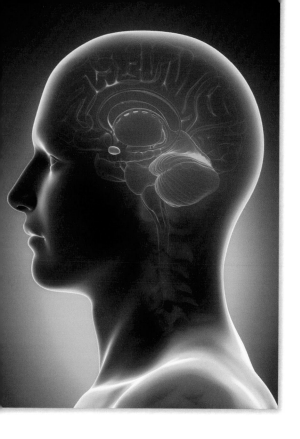

This picture shows the location of the amygdala in the human brain. The amygdala is believed to have a connection to implicit racial bias.

amygdala activity upon seeing African American faces when White participants were asked to sort images of faces by race. Another study led by researchers at Tufts and New York University found that the amygdala became active when White participants were asked to make superficial judgments about pictures of Black faces. From these, scientists have theorized that the enhanced amygdala activation represents implicit racial bias or, more specifically, an unconscious fear response to African Americans, particularly men.

Yet one of the few fMRI studies that tested both Black and White subjects has shown that African Americans can also have increased amygdala activity upon seeing an unfamiliar African American face. This result suggests that African Americans can have implicit racial bias toward their own race. "I think the results are very specific to being raised in this society where the portrayal of African Americans is not very positive, on average," says study leader Matthew Lieberman of the University of California, Los Angeles. "It suggests that those cultural messages are not harmless."[29] In other words, the bias is culturally learned.

Context Matters

The amygdala doesn't always fire in White participants upon seeing unfamiliar Black faces. Researchers have found that when study subjects are given a specific context for looking at images of African Americans, the amygdala does not show the same heightened activity at all. In one study, Fiske showed White participants a series of photos with Black and White faces. They were given two seconds to answer one of three questions: whether the subject of the photo was over age twenty-one, whether the subject had a gray dot on his or her face, or whether the subject liked a particular vegetable.

The results showed that when the participants had to assess the age of the person in the photo, their amygdala activity spiked when the picture was of a Black person. However, when participants were asked to assess whether the person in the photo had a gray dot on his or her face or whether the person liked a certain vegetable, the amygdala activity was at the same level

Virtual Body Swapping

Can virtual reality help overcome implicit racial bias? Some scientists believe so. Researchers Mel Slater and Manos Tsakiris conducted a series of experiments in which they used virtual reality (VR) and optical illusions on White participants to create the perception that the participants had darker skin tone.

In the first part of the experiment, the subjects had their real hand and cheek stroked while gazing at a video-recorded image of an African American having the same body part stroked. This illusion tricked the subjects' brains into thinking they are the person they're seeing. Next, the participants donned a VR headset to be fully immersed into the body with a darker skin tone. As a control, the subjects took an implicit bias test to assess their level of unconscious bias both before and after the experiment.

The researchers found that the subjects showed significantly reduced implicit racial bias after the virtual experience. Although VR can't give the genuine experience of a person of color, "seeing the world from the point of view of another person, literally having their body, may change empathy regarding certain kinds of people," says Slater. "So I think it could be something that's for good in the world."

Quoted in Alissa Zhu, "Can Virtual Bodyswapping Help Fight Racial Prejudice?," *Popular Science*, January 19, 2015. www.popsci.com.

as when participants saw White faces. The team concluded that when participants judged the people in the photos as individuals, they didn't react to Black faces any differently than White ones. It was only when they assigned the faces to a particular social category that they had a response along racial lines, even though the category related to age rather than race.

Several similar studies have validated these results. In one, White participants did not show increased amygdala activity upon viewing the face of well-known Black celebrities. In another, the amygdala sparked in White participants when asked to categorize a mixed-race crowd by race—but didn't when asked to classify the same crowd by sports jersey. These studies demonstrate that the brain can change the way it reacts to faces of a different race depending on the social conditions, suggesting that implicit racial bias is not set in stone.

Broader In-Groups

Our strong preference for in-group members also weakens the argument that implicit racial bias is hardwired. Studies consistently indicate that racial bias fades when people consider a member

In one study, researchers showed White participants a series of photos with Black and White faces. They found that when participants judged the people in the photos as individuals, they didn't react to Black faces any differently than White ones.

of a racial out-group as part of their in-group. Psychologist Jay Van Bavel conducted a series of experiments to examine this effect.

In one study, Van Bavel told White participants they would be on a team and asked them to memorize the photos of their teammates' faces, some of whom were White and others Black. Afterward, he had the participants take a computerized bias test in which they were shown photos of their team members along with a picture of a different racially mixed team. The participants showed no sign of unconscious bias when seeing photos of the Black members of their own team, although they did show some bias when seeing Black members of the other team.

In a second study, Van Bavel scanned White participants' brains as they looked at photos of their teammates and the opposing team. He found that their amygdalae showed heightened activity when looking at photos of the opposing team, regardless of race. This result suggested that racial bias had been overridden by the perception of threat from a different out-group—the other team. A third study showed that when White participants were shown photos of their Black teammates, their brain activity activated in regions associated with feelings of camaraderie rather than bias. "The results suggest that when we share some kind of identity with a group of people, we automatically and immediately feel positively toward them, regardless of race,"[30] says Van Bavel. Indeed, the larger implication of these studies is that we may be able to diminish implicit racial bias by thinking of people of other races as in-group members due to another shared relationship—or better yet, that we're all inherently part of the same team.

> "When we share some kind of identity with a group of people, we automatically and immediately feel positively toward them, regardless of race."[30]
>
> —Jay Van Bavel, psychologist

No Amygdala Response in Kids

Kids demonstrate implicit racial bias at a young age, but they don't show the same amygdala response as adults. In a small but important fMRI study from the University of Illinois, researchers observed amygdala activity in thirty-two African American and European American children, ranging from age four to sixteen. None of the children showed an elevated amygdala response to African American faces until adolescence. According to behavioral and data scientist Pragya Agarwal, these results "quash any suggestions that we are born 'racists' and that we have racial prejudice in our nature."[31] Rather, the results point to how environmental cues affect how we absorb stereotypes and biases as we age.

The study also validated research showing that by broadening our in-group we can reduce racial bias. The youth who had more exposure to diverse races among their peer group had less amygdala activity in response to African American faces than the other children in the study. Many experts see these results as confirming other tests showing that people in cross-racial households display

WHISTLING VIVALDI

Many people of color often go out of their way to signal to White people that they're in-group members in the hopes of avoiding the negative consequences of implicit bias. Famously, when African American journalist Brent Staples was a student at the University of Chicago, he noticed that White people reacted to him fearfully when he went for a walk at night. They moved out of his path, clutched their bags, or avoided eye contact with him.

To put people at ease—and protect himself from any backlash from their fear—he began whistling Vivaldi or other familiar melodies as he walked. The attitude of White passersby changed immediately. The tension drained from their bodies, and some even smiled at him, presumably now seeing him as an educated or upper-class Black individual rather than a stereotypical threat.

While such an approach may put people at ease, Stanford University psychologist Claude Steele notes that it comes at a great psychic cost to people of color. Feeling pressured to prove you don't conform to a relevant stereotype—also known as stereotype threat—puts a heavy and unfair burden on the people being stereotyped, significantly enhancing their anxiety and stress.

Researchers have found that younger children do not display an elevated amygdala response to African American faces, and that this elevated response does not appear until adolescence. This suggests that racial bias comes from environmental influences, not genetics.

much weaker signs of implicit bias. "The more positive contact we have with people from different ethnic groups, the less likely we are to form the notion of threat associated with unfamiliar faces, and the less likely we are to imbibe the stereotypical messages that we receive from words and images in the media,"[32] says Agarwal.

Overriding Impulses

Scientists are further encouraged by neuroimaging studies showing that White Americans with positive attitudes toward African Americans use the self-control region of the brain when judging African American images that typically trigger racial stereotypes and bias. Such results suggest that the brain has the power to override implicit bias and allow individuals to make decisions that are less influenced by prejudice.

The bottom line is that we shouldn't underestimate our brain's capacity to adapt. Implicit racial bias may be born of a biological impulse to categorize and reinforced by an environment filled with racially biased messages, but the brain has the ability to understand its errors and push against them. It won't be easy, but we can change our biased ways—if we have the will.

CHAPTER FIVE

Fighting Implicit Racial Bias

"This is the most emotionally challenging thing I've ever done,"[33] admits Henry Littell, reflecting on his efforts to learn about racial bias. Littell, a student at Glenthorne High School in South London, is one of twenty-four kids featured in the documentary *The School That Tried to End Racism*. The film tracks an intense and ambitious school program intended to detect and reduce racism and implicit racial bias in students.

Littell may well speak for anyone who has taken a candid look at their racial biases. Few people want to admit they harbor prejudiced or stereotypical racial views, even ones that only exist in their subconscious. It feels ugly, wrong, and at odds with how we see ourselves. And yet admitting to our own implicit bias is the most essential step in fighting it. We cannot hope to reduce implicit bias's impact on society without first acknowledging that bias exists within and around us.

Social psychologist and author Beverly Daniel Tatum likens implicit racial bias to smog, saying:

> You sometimes hear people say there is not a prejudiced bone in my body. But . . . we might gently say to them check again. That if we have all been breathing in smog, we can't help but have our thinking shaped by

it somehow. As a consequence, we all have work to do. Whether you identify as a person of color, whether you identify as a white person, it doesn't matter. We all have been exposed to misinformation that we have to think critically about.[34]

Since the world witnessed the horrific murder of George Floyd in May 2020 at the hands of police officer Derek Chauvin, interest in implicit racial bias has exploded. Even if a painful exploration awaits, more and more people want to understand their own biases, take steps to reduce them, and contain the harm. But where to begin the process? Some say testing your level of implicit racial bias is the first move.

The 2020 murder of George Floyd spurred increased public interest in implicit racial bias. Here, a protester holds a picture of Floyd at a 2020 protest in Washington, DC.

The Race Implicit Association Test

In the 1990s Mahzarin Banaji and Anthony Greenwald developed a test designed to measure an individual's implicit preference for specific racial or social groups over others. The Implicit Association Test (IAT) is based on the theory that people quickly associate certain words with certain concepts when the two things are already linked in their mind. For example, most people associate the word *flower* with positive things, such as beauty, fragrance, spring, and so forth. On the other hand, we are more likely to associate *insects* with negative things, such as creepy, stinging, biting, and so on. When timed, most people are quicker to pair *flowers* with positive words than with negative words and *insects* with negative words because we regularly make these associations in our mind. But it takes longer to pair flowers with negative words and insects with positive words because we're not used to these associations.

The race IAT uses this model to measure the extent to which individuals associate African Americans and White Americans with pleasant or negative concepts. The IAT measures test takers' reaction times as they sort computerized images of Black and White faces with positive or negative words. The researchers theorize that people who are quicker to associate White or Black faces with positive words have an implicit preference for that race—the faster the association, the stronger the preference.

Located on Harvard University's Project Implicit site, the test has been taken well over 20 million times. Researchers have found that roughly 75 percent of those who take the race IAT have an automatic White preference. Many people who firmly believe themselves to be egalitarian, including Banaji and Greenwald themselves, have been surprised and disappointed to learn of their bias.

The test designers emphasize, however, that a score showing a preference for a particular race doesn't mean that an individual is racist or prejudiced. Rather, it suggests that the person's racial preference may unconsciously influence his or her actions and cause the person to treat nonpreferred racial groups unfairly. The hope is that with this knowledge, people can remain vigilant against showing unfair bias.

Organizations Fighting Implicit Bias

Thousands of businesses and institutions across the nation are seeking ways to diminish bias in their organizations. Starbucks, Google, and countless other companies have hired diversity experts to provide antibias training programs for staff as well as for executives. Hospitals and medical schools are doing the same for students, medical staff, and administrators, as are schools, from nursery through graduate programs. However, many social scientists are skeptical about the effectiveness of antibias training. "There is ample evidence that training alone does not change attitudes or behavior, or not by much and not for long,"[35] sociologists Frank Dobbin and Alexandra Kalev wrote in a 2018 study.

CRITICISMS OF THE IMPLICIT ASSOCIATION TEST

Despite its wide usage as a measure of implicit bias, the Implicit Association Test is heavily criticized in the social science community. Many scientists dispute its reliability, given that score results can greatly vary depending on multiple factors, including an individual's mood when taking the test, understanding of the task, facility with computer buttons, and desire to create a good impression. The test also might measure explicit biases as well as implicit biases.

"If the measure is an amalgamation of many things (one of which is purportedly implicit bias), how can we know which of those things is responsible for a (weak) correlation with behavior?" says James Jaccard, a New York University researcher.

Quoted in German Lopez, "For Years This Popular Test Measured Anyone's Bias. But It Might Not Work After All," Vox, March 7, 2017. www.vox.com.

Diversity experts and scientists agree that organizations genuinely committed to diminishing implicit bias must prepare for a sustained battle on multiple fronts. The organization should have a diversity strategy in which antibias training is merely a part. A diversity strategy aims to increase the number of racial minorities within the organization. "The way to get people to change their stereotypes about other groups is to have them work side by side with members of other groups as equals,"[36] says Dobbin.

Further, organizations must take a hard look at their operational structures and change systems that promote racial bias and inequality. For example, the Oakland Police Department changed its foot-pursuit policies. Instead of chasing a suspect into a dark, unfamiliar place, officers were required to stop, set up a perimeter, and wait for backup. Implicit bias expert Jennifer L. Eberhardt says this change gave officers time for rational decision-making instead of knee-jerk, biased reactions. After adopting this policy, Oakland officer-involved shootings dropped from eight or nine per year to eight across five years.

> "The way to get people to change their stereotypes about other groups is to have them work side by side with members of other groups as equals."[36]
>
> —Frank Dobbin, social scientist

Nextdoor, the social platform for neighborhood communities, also made changes to decrease biased actions. The platform was being used to call attention to "suspicious" people in the neighborhood—people often identified only as "Black" without other details suggesting suspicious activity. To reduce biased reporting, Nextdoor required users to precisely describe the suspicious activity and give a detailed description of the person and the person's clothes to minimize the risk of misidentification. Biased reports immediately plunged.

In the medical industry, a state medical center in Ohio partnered with Mid-Ohio Food Collective, one of the largest food banks in the country, to help low-income state residents receive fresh produce and other healthy foods. The program allows medical providers to write a "food prescription" for patients who face

Cognitive Shortcuts That Can Reinforce Implicit Racial Bias

Psychologists Daniel Kahneman and Amos Tversky identified over twenty cognitive shortcuts that can reinforce implicit racial bias. To reduce implicit racial bias, we must avoid falling prey to shortcuts such as the following:

- **Confirmation bias:** when we look only for information that confirms a preexisting belief.
- **Availability cascade:** when we believe that a certain thing is true simply because we've heard about it more, not because it is actually true.
- **The horn effect:** when we allow our perception of a person to be influenced by a single negative trait.
- **Attentional bias:** when we pay attention to certain behaviors while ignoring others.
- **Fundamental attribution bias:** when we attribute an individual's behavior to a stereotype but attribute similar behavior of our own to external factors.

food insecurity and have chronic health conditions—of whom a disproportionate number are people of color.

This program provides a solution to patients who cannot afford to follow their medical provider's advice to eat more healthily. Equally important, it makes a point to medical providers who might be biased to believe patients of color won't comply with their medical advice due to obstinacy. As one doctor notes, "I've had a patient tell me that she's now able to afford her insulin because she doesn't have to spend as much on food."[37]

Hope for the Future

Some say our best hope of reducing implicit racial bias lies with children. Kids may show signs of implicit racial bias at an early age, but studies show those who have cross-racial relationships

Teaching About Race Promotes Understanding

A majority of US adults believes that teaching about the history of race in America helps students gain an understanding of other people's experiences. This is the finding of a CBS News/YouGov survey conducted in February 2022. A smaller percentage of survey participants believes that such teaching leads to greater racial tolerance but even fewer are of the opinion that it makes people less tolerant.

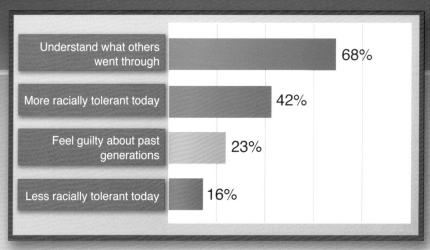

Think Teaching About Race in America Makes Students . . .

Understand what others went through	68%
More racially tolerant today	42%
Feel guilty about past generations	23%
Less racially tolerant today	16%

Source: Fred Backus and Anthony Salvanto, "Big Majorities Reject Book Bans—CBS News Poll," CBS News/YouGov, February 22, 2022. www.cbsnews.com.

display significantly less bias. That's why many experts urge parents and educators to give children the knowledge and tools to fight racism, stereotyping, and implicit bias as early as possible.

Many White parents take a color-blind approach to race. They teach their children that all people are equal regardless of color or race but don't discuss the issue much beyond this. But the color-blind approach ignores the experiences of people of color and minimizes the societal racial inequities and disparities. It also fails to counterbalance the subtle or not-so-subtle messages about race that children pick up from their environment or the media. In the end, studies show that this approach has little effect on implicit bias.

Experts say that to reduce implicit bias in children, it is crucial that parents explicitly discuss race, racism, and stereotypes.

Research has found that children who have candid conversations about race with their parents show less racial bias than kids whose parents take the color-blind approach. Other research shows that reading positive stories about people of color can help counteract stereotyping and reduce bias.

Many schools are taking a proactive approach to teaching children about implicit bias. Tens of thousands of teachers have downloaded an antibias program developed by the Southern Poverty Law Center's Teaching Tolerance (now Learning for Justice) unit. Countless schools have developed and adopted their own antibias curriculums. But a few schools have gone to extraordinary lengths to tackle bias—with promising results.

The School That Tried to End Racism

Glenthorne High School, the London school featured in the documentary *The School That Tried to End Racism*, ran an experimental antibias program. Students spent three weeks learning about bias, honestly unpacking their racial views, examining their racial identities, and listening and learning from each other's experiences and perspectives. The full group was composed of twenty-four students of various races and ethnicities. Part of the curriculum involved temporarily separating kids by race into different "affinity groups" to discuss racial issues without feeling inhibited by the presence of other races—a move that was considered somewhat controversial.

Issues of race and racial bias were incorporated into regular study areas. For example, in biology the students learned that humans are genetically 99.9 percent the same. In visiting London's National Portrait Gallery, they observed that very few portraits of people of color were featured, although people of color have lived in the United Kingdom for centuries. In sports class, they ran a race in which the starting line for each student depended on the answer to questions such as "Is English your parents' first language?" or "Have your parents ever warned you about racism?"[38]

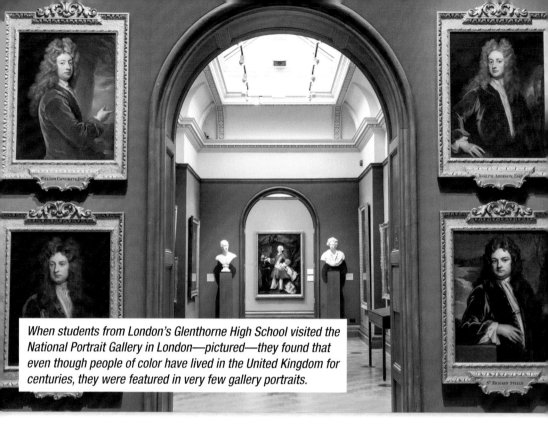

When students from London's Glenthorne High School visited the National Portrait Gallery in London—pictured—they found that even though people of color have lived in the United Kingdom for centuries, they were featured in very few gallery portraits.

The fewer race-related issues students had to deal with in their lives, the closer their starting line was to the finish line—a striking 3-D lesson about privilege.

The program administrators used the IAT to measure the students' progress. At the start of the program, the IAT results showed that the vast majority of the students had a White preference. When the children retook the test at the end, the class erupted into cheers when the teacher announced that almost all received a neutral score. But perhaps even more important, students of all races expressed how much more comfortable they were talking about racial issues with their peers.

The enhanced comfort level in talking about race is key. While kids may have racially diverse friendships in childhood, they tend to gravitate toward their own racial groups in adolescence. "They'll end the friendship rather than wade in and have a dialogue,"[39] says Mariama Richards, an African American "equity practitioner" who oversaw the Glenthorne program and runs similar ones in schools in New York City. Helping children talk openly about race may be central to maintaining interracial friendships through adolescence and reducing implicit bias in adulthood.

What Can You Do?

All individuals—no matter their racial group—can do their part in reducing implicit racial bias and making the world a more equitable place. The first step is acknowledging our biases and making a conscious effort to work on them without defensiveness or shame. Experts say that examining our biases will feel uncomfortable, but it's vital to forward progress. "This is hard work," says psychologist Jade Wu. "It's not something we can do by shutting up and staying in our comfort zones."[40]

Resisting stereotypes is also critical to fighting implicit bias. One way to do this is by consciously viewing every person as an individual. Our fast brain may immediately sort people into broad categories, but our conscious mind knows that every person is unique. Each of us has our own stories, dreams, fears, interests, and goals. Make a practice of looking for the shared humanity in someone different from you.

We can further resist stereotypes by challenging our assumptions. The brown-skinned person with the stethoscope around her neck might be the doctor, not the assistant. The student with a foreign-sounding name might be a third-generation American. The White businessman might be educating himself on racial issues to be a better ally. The young Black man strolling down the street is probably on his way home from the store, thinking about what's for dinner.

Educate yourself about different racial groups. Innumerable books, magazines, blogs, documentaries, podcasts, and articles explore the history, lives, and experiences of people of color in this country. Fight negative stereotypes by learning about the achievements and day-to-day experiences of people in different racial groups. Consider where the media might be giving you a distorted or one-sided picture of a particular group and research the bigger picture.

Don't shy away from opportunities to develop genuine relationships with people of different races. Having friends with varied backgrounds and experiences is crucial to understanding other people's realities, deepening our insights, and diminishing biases.

Above all, it's essential not to let mistakes stop us. Challenging implicit bias is a lifelong journey, although hopefully, we will see improvement within ourselves and in society along the way. "We can't promise to be perfect, but we can promise to remain open to learning,"[41] says organizational psychologist Nancy Doyle. Or in the words of Bright, a student in *The School That Tried to Stop Racism*, "The [world] is never going to be fully unracist, but we might as well try, right?"[42]

SOURCE NOTES

Introduction: An Insidious Harm

1. Melissa DePino (@missydepino), "The police were called because these men hadn't ordered anything," Twitter, April 12, 2018. https://twitter.com.
2. Kevin Johnson, "Starbucks CEO: Reprehensible Outcome in Philadelphia Incident," Starbucks Stories & News, April 14, 2018. https://stories.starbucks.com.
3. Quoted in *Washington Post*, "Can You Change Implicit Bias?," May 25, 2018. www.washingtonpost.com.

Chapter One: The Roots of Bias

4. Quoted in Paul Bisceglio, "Your Stories of Battling Unconscious Bias," *The Atlantic*, June 7, 2017. www.theatlantic.com.
5. Art Markman, "You End Up Believing What You Want to Believe," *Ulterior Motives* (blog), *Psychology Today*, July 1, 2011. www.psychologytoday.com.
6. Quoted in Association for Psychological Science, "People with Low Self-Esteem Show More Signs of Prejudice," February 23, 2011. www.psychologicalscience.org.
7. Quoted in Kathleen Osta and Hugh Vasquez, "Implicit Bias and Structural Racialization," National Equity Project. www.nationalequityproject.org.

Chapter Two: How Implicit Racial Bias Develops

8. Quoted in Debby Irving, *Waking Up White: And Finding Myself in the Story of Race*. Cambridge, MA: Elephant, 2014, p. 11.
9. Irving, *Waking Up White*, p. 14.
10. Irving, *Waking Up White*, p. 14.
11. Irving, *Waking Up White*, p. 14.
12. Quoted in Amanda Armstrong, "Bias Starts as Early as Preschool, but Can Be Unlearned," Edutopia, June 4, 2019. www.edutopia.org.
13. Allison Skinner, "How Do Children Acquire Prejudices?," *Catching Bias* (blog), *Psychology Today*, November 1, 2019. www.psychologytoday.com.

14. Jennifer L. Eberhardt, *Biased: Uncovering the Hidden Prejudice That Shapes What We See, Think, and Do*. New York: Viking, 2019, pp. 3–4.
15. Eberhardt, *Biased*, p. 4.
16. Quoted in Heather Greenwood Davis, "Is Your Child's Extra Screen Time Creating Racial Bias?," National Geographic, April 7, 2021. www.nationalgeographic.com.

Chapter Three: The Destructive Effects of Implicit Racial Bias

17. Quoted in Lucy Tompkins, "Here's What You Need to Know About Elijah McClain's Death," *New York Times*, October 19, 2021. www.nytimes.com.
18. Quoted in American Psychological Association, "People See Black Men as Larger, More Threatening than Same-Sized White Men," March 13, 2017. www.apa.org.
19. Tompkins, "Here's What You Need to Know About Elijah McClain's Death."
20. Sarah E. Fiarman, "Unconscious Bias: When Good Intentions Aren't Enough," ASCD, November 1, 2016. www.ascd.org.
21. Fiarman, "Unconscious Bias."
22. Quoted in Jillian Olinger et al., "Challenging Race as Risk: How Implicit Bias Undermines Housing Opportunity in America—and What We Can Do About It," Kirwan Institute for the Study of Race and Ethnicity, 2017. http://kirwaninstitute.osu.edu.
23. Quoted in Bob Salsberg and Angeliki Kastanis, "Analysis: Blacks Largely Left Out of High-Paying Jobs, Government Data Shows," *USA Today*, April 4, 2018. https://eu.usatoday.com.
24. Quoted in National Academies of Sciences, Engineering, and Medicine, "Minorities More Likely to Receive Lower-Quality Health Care, Regardless of Income and Insurance Coverage," March 20, 2002. www.nationalacademies.org.
25. Quoted in Jordan Reed, "Understanding Racial Microaggression and Its Effects on Mental Health," Pfizer, 2022. www.pfizer.com.

Chapter Four: Is Implicit Racial Bias Hardwired?

26. Quoted in Leigh Mingle, "Implicit Bias: Sharing Our Stories," Ensemble Learning, October 19, 2019. https://ensemblelearning.org.
27. Susan Fiske, "Look Twice," Greater Good, June 1, 2008. https://greatergood.berkeley.edu.

28. Mina Cikara and Jay Van Bavel, "The Flexibility of Racial Bias," *Scientific American*, Summer 2021, p. 39.
29. Quoted in Anna Gosline, "Brain Scans Reveal Racial Biases," *New Scientist*, May 8, 2005. www.newscientist.com.
30. Quoted in Eureka Alert, "Racial Biases Fade Away Toward Members of Your Own Group," March 23, 2009. www.eurekalert.org.
31. Pragya Agarwal, *Sway: Unravelling Unconscious Bias*. London: Bloomsbury Sigma, 2020, p. 84.
32. Agarwal, *Sway*, p. 85.

Chapter Five: Fighting Implicit Racial Bias

33. Quoted in *The School That Tried to End Racism*, June 25, 2020. www.channel4.com.
34. Quoted in PBS, "Interview with Beverly Daniel Tatum," 2003. www.pbs.org.
35. Quoted in Amanda Abrams, "What Anti-Bias Training Can—and Can't—Accomplish in the Workplace," *Journal of Accountancy*, January 1, 2021. www.journalofaccountancy.com.
36. Quoted in Julia Belluz, "Companies Like Starbucks Love Anti-Bias Training. But It Doesn't Work—and May Backfire," Vox, May 29, 2018. www.vox.com.
37. Quoted in Susannah Elliot Kistler, "Ohio State Invests in Ending Central Ohio Food Insecurity," Wexner Medical Center, Ohio State University, August 31, 2021. https://wexnermedical.osu.edu.
38. Quoted in *The School That Tried to End Racism*, episode 2.
39. Quoted in Lisa Miller, "Can Bias Be Stopped in the Third Grade?," The Cut, May 19, 2015. www.thecut.com.
40. Jade Wu, "How Being Less Defensive About Racism Will Help You Grow," Quick and Dirty Tips, September 18, 2020. www.quickanddirtytips.com.
41. Nancy Doyle, "Tackling Implicit Bias: Does the 'Woke' Movie Business Have an Inclusion Problem?," *Forbes*, January 16, 2020. www.forbes.com.
42. Quoted in *The School That Tried to End Racism*.

ORGANIZATIONS AND WEBSITES

Institute for Humane Education
https://humaneeducation.org
The Institute for Humane Education teaches students on a range of interconnected global and ethical topics. It offers an assortment of online and offline workshops, programs, lessons, and articles for young adults. The institute is affiliated with Antioch University.

Learning for Justice
www.learningforjustice.org
Learning for Justice, formerly known as Teaching Tolerance, was founded by the Southern Poverty Law Center in 1991. Its goal is to advance the human rights of all people by providing children with the tools to fight White supremacy and foster social justice. The website offers articles, activities, stories, poems, and publications for students in kindergarten through high school.

PBS LearningMedia
https://pbslearningmedia.org
PBS LearningMedia is a free digital content library for students in kindergarten through high school. The website offers a collection of interactive videos and lessons on race, racism, and implicit bias, in addition to numerous other topics.

Project Implicit
www.projectimplicit.net
Project Implicit transforms academic research on implicit bias into practical applications that address diversity and help improve decision-making. The site hosts the Implicit Association Test, which helps people assess their implicit bias.

TED
www.ted.com
TED is a nonprofit organization committed to spreading ideas. The website has numerous video-recorded talks on implicit bias, race, and racism. The organization aims to help people understand how we can change ourselves and the world.

FOR FURTHER RESEARCH

Books

Robin DiAngelo, *White Fragility: Why It's So Hard for White People to Talk About Race*. Boston, MA: Beacon, 2018.

Tiffany Jewell, *This Book Is Anti-Racist: 20 Lessons on How to Wake Up, Take Action, and Do the Work*. Minneapolis, MN: Frances Lincoln Children's Books, 2020.

Ibram X. Kendi, *How to Be an Antiracist*. New York: Random House, 2019.

Ijeoma Oluo, *So You Want to Talk About Race*. New York: Seal, 2018.

Beverly Daniel Tatum, *Why Are All the Black Kids Sitting Together in the Cafeteria?* New York: Basic Books, 2017.

Internet Sources

Tasminda Dhaliwal et al., "Education Bias Is Associated with Racial Disparities in Student Achievement and Discipline," *The Brown Center Chalkboard* (blog), Brookings Institution, July 20, 2020. www.brookings.edu.

Allison Felt, "Pulling Back the Curtain on Racial Bias," Stanford Graduate School of Business, July 16, 2020. www.gsb.stanford.edu.

Governing, "Implicit Racial Bias Leads to Inequitable Health Care," November 29, 2021. www.governing.com.

Meryl Davids Landau, "To Overcome Unconscious Bias You Must Realize It's Deeply Ingrained in Your Brain," *Prevention*, April 7, 2021. www.prevention.com.

Ari Shapiro, "'There Is No Neutral': 'Nice White People' Can Still Be Complicit in a Racist Society," NPR, June 9, 2020. www.npr.org.

Sentencing Project, "Report to the United Nations on Racial Disparities in the U.S. Criminal Justice System," April 19, 2018. www.sentencingproject.org.

Vishnu Sridhara, "A Way to Move Past Implicit Bias," *Time*, July 20, 2015. https://time.com.

INDEX

Note: Boldface page numbers indicate illustrations.